BEI GRIN MACHT SICH IHR
WISSEN BEZAHLT

- Wir veröffentlichen Ihre Hausarbeit,
  Bachelor- und Masterarbeit

- Ihr eigenes eBook und Buch -
  weltweit in allen wichtigen Shops

- Verdienen Sie an jedem Verkauf

Jetzt bei www.GRIN.com hochladen
und kostenlos publizieren

Bibliografische Information der Deutschen Nationalbibliothek:

Die Deutsche Bibliothek verzeichnet diese Publikation in der Deutschen National-
bibliografie; detaillierte bibliografische Daten sind im Internet über http://dnb.d-
nb.de/ abrufbar.

Impressum:

Copyright © 2009 GRIN Verlag, Open Publishing GmbH
Druck und Bindung: Books on Demand GmbH, Norderstedt Germany
ISBN: 9783656912088

Dieses Buch bei GRIN:

http://www.grin.com/de/e-book/140792/conventional-gender-roles-in-viginia-woolf-
s-to-the-lighthouse

Agnieszka Siedlik

Conventional Gender Roles in Viginia Woolf's "To the Lighthouse"

GRIN Verlag

GRIN - Your knowledge has value

Der GRIN Verlag publiziert seit 1998 wissenschaftliche Arbeiten von Studenten, Hochschullehrern und anderen Akademikern als eBook und gedrucktes Buch. Die Verlagswebsite www.grin.com ist die ideale Plattform zur Veröffentlichung von Hausarbeiten, Abschlussarbeiten, wissenschaftlichen Aufsätzen, Dissertationen und Fachbüchern.

Besuchen Sie uns im Internet:

http://www.grin.com/

http://www.facebook.com/grincom

http://www.twitter.com/grin_com

Universität Regensburg
Institut für Anglistik und Amerikanistik
Wintersemester 2008/2009
Proseminar: Modernist Prose Writings

Conventional Gender Roles in *To the Lighthouse*

The Influence on the Characters and Virginia Woolf

Agnieszka Siedlik

Outline

1. Introduction: Virginia Woolf's *To the Lighthouse*

Virginia Woolf's novel *To the Lighthouse* was published in 1927. Considering the period of its composition, it is not surprising that it was written in the literary genre of modernism. Woolf uses an anonymous narrator, who describes the characters subjectively in the third person. As there is a constant switch from the thoughts and feelings of one character to another, it is possible to see the real meaningless of life, an existential angst that each of the protagonists tries to overcome. Woolf deliberately uses characters that are quite similar to real people from her own childhood during the first World War, when England had an fairly stratified class system marked by extreme social differentiation, especially for men and women. The novel's setting mirrors her life, as well: the story takes place both before and after the Great War.

I will begin my analysis by describing all the gender roles in *To the Lighthouse* and attempt to show how they influence each character. I will place particular emphasis on Mr. and Mrs Ramsay, as well as Lily Briscoe, in order to demonstrate their way of life and their problems. I will then examine Virginia Woolf's own family and era, for they constitute an archetype of a family living under the class system characteristic of the time. At this point, I will also demonstrate how Virginia Woolf's parents served as models for the characters of Mr. and Mrs. Ramsay. Furthermore, I will focus on Lily Briscoe and illustrate how she tries to adopt some of the Ramsay's positive traits and gradually discovers her own female identity. To conclude, I will compare Virginia Woolf with Lily Briscoe to show that they are quite alike, and that her family resembles the Ramsays significantly. "To the Lighthouse," as Bowlby writes, "represents a darker insight into the woman's `structurally untenable position` within male-dominated society,

subtly undermining any complacently `androgynous` ideal unity"
(8).

2. Important gender roles in *To the Lighthouse*

2.1 Mrs. Ramsay

Each character in *To the Lighthouse* has own individual
gender roles. Mr. and Mrs. Ramsay are the most prominent
characters to do so: Mrs. Ramsay, for instance, is the mother of
eight children, as well as a loving woman of striking appearance.
We eventually discover, in my opinion, that this beautiful exterior
does not mirror her true inner feelings and concerns. As a woman
of the older generation, Mrs. Ramsay's world and point of view are
build on tradition. Her family is the most important thing for her,
and she pities those who do not have a family and must live on
their own. Consequently, she tries to arrange marriages between
her children and the guests who stay with them in their summer
house. In her opinion, it is the most important thing for a woman
to marry, because otherwise she will certainly be unhappy: "they
all must marry [...] there could be no disputing this [...] an
unmarried woman has missed the best of life." (Woolf, *To the
Lighthouse* 43).

We discover that Mrs. Ramsay holds family to be important
not only because of tradition, but also because she has no desire
to deal with the new form of life called modernism. According to
her, modernism would harm or even destroy the scheme and
harmony she tries to establish. When her family and a couple of
guests gather together peacefully around a table: these are the
moments that arouse the most happiness in her. To my mind, the
reason for this is that thus Mrs. Ramsay is satisfied that, in this

act of fellowship, she creates something that modernism and the changing times cannot take away from her. In the following passage she conveys one of these sensations:

> [...] all of which rising in this profound stillness [...] seemed now for no special reason to stay there like a smoke, like a fume rising upwards, holding them safe together. Nothing needed to be said; nothing could be said. There it was, all round them. It partook, she felt, [...]; as she had already felt about something different once before that afternoon; there is coherence in things, a stability; something, she meant, is immune from change, and shines out [...] in the face of the flowing, the fleeting, the spectral, like a ruby; so that again tonight she had the feeling she had had once today already, of peace, of rest. Of such moments, she thought, the thing is made that remains for ever after. This would remain. (Woolf, *To the Lighthouse* 85)

Mrs. Ramsay's main ambition is to protect her youngest son James, her husband, and especially her male guests. She encourages her son's hope for going to the lighthouse, despite the view of her husband and Charles Tansley, who want the child to think realistically. Their opinions sometimes destroy Mrs. Ramsay's aim to protect her children; nevertheless, she shelters both her husband and all the other men, who normally do not deserve her generosity. She thinks that men need constant support and sympathy, and that they particularly need to be reassured by women:

> Indeed she had the whole of the other sex under her protection; for reasons she could not explain, for their chivalry and valour, for the fact that they negotiated treaties, ruled India, controlled finance; finally for an attitude towards herself which no woman could fail to feel or to find agreeable, something trustful. Childlike, reverential. (Woolf, *To the Lighthouse* 9)

Mrs. Ramsay sticks to her belief that men are very important in people's lives, especially for women. Therefore she "pitied men always as if they lacked something – women never, as if they had something" (Woolf, *To the Lighthouse* 70). Although Mrs. Ramsay is convinced that women should marry and be under their husbands standing, she knows also that women wield a female power (Lily Briscoe is the only one who utilizes this female power, as I will describe presently). I gather she is aware that not everyone will cope with this conventional life, but she does not allow herself to be entrapped within traditional gender roles. Despite her sense of duty in marriage, I believe there a moments where Mrs. Ramsay longs to escape her mother or wife role, to free herself from all those difficult emotions: "she often felt she was nothing but a sponge sopped full of human emotions." (Woolf, *To the Lighthouse* 29)

Finally, Mrs. Ramsay is a woman who has an almost abnormal need to help other people, even though they do not want it themselves. Her motive for doing so is her desire to be thought of as a woman of high society, a woman who is able to supply everybody's need:

> For her own self-satisfaction was it that she wished so instinctively to help, to give, that people might say of her, `O Mrs Ramsay! Dear Mrs Ramsay [...] Mrs Ramsay, of course!` and need her and send for her and admire her? (Woolf, *To the Lighthouse* 37)

Supported by her external appearance of happiness and beauty, as I stated previously, she also wants other people to regard her as a totally happy and satisfied woman. She wants a lot of woman to want to be like her, to step into her shoes. But her outer beauty diverges greatly from her inner life, which is sometimes fraught with sadness and a lack of fulfilment.

2.2 Mr. Ramsay

Mr. Ramsay is a man of the older generation, and he never diverges from his stereotypical gender role. In his estimation, the most important thing for a man is to work hard and become someone very important. He is a prominent metaphysical philosopher, and he knows that he is respected by others, but this is not enough. He wants to be the best, so that he will be admired and remembered by future generations. He compares a man's career with the alphabet: those on the lowest echelon are marked by the letter A, the worst; and a man who has achieved the letter Z has reached the pinnacle of success. Mr. Ramsay judges himself to have "reached Q. Very few people in the whole of England ever reach Q. [...] Still, if he could reach R it would be something. Here at least was Q" (Woolf, *To the Lighthouse* 30/31). It seems that Mr. Ramsay is not able to free himself from stress and pressure. He is constantly pondering about how to be more and more successful, and he often fears that his work lacks worth and meaning. "In that flash of darkness he heard people saying - he was a failure - that R was beyond him. He would never reach R. On to R, once more R- " (Woolf, *To the Lighthouse* 31).

Although Mr. Ramsay serves, in many respects, as Mrs. Ramsay's opposite, the fear of failure is one of the features that both of them possess. Obviously, Mr. Ramsay is very ambitious regarding his work, as he ought to be for a man of his age. To my mind, however, sometimes he would like to free himself from this professional burden. On the one hand, he is willing to set the world on fire; on the other, he would like to be accepted and adored by people for the things he has already achieved. But he cannot allow himself to reveal these feelings, for he is a man with huge commitments. Of the two, it is Mrs. Ramsay who occasionally worries about her husband's true inner feelings. In her eyes, Mr. Ramsay and other men seem to lack the capacity of perceiving the beauty in nature and the world right before their eyes. "Did he notice the flowers? No. Did he notice the view? No. Did he even notice his own daughter's beauty, or whether there was pudding on his plate or roast beef? He would sit at table with them like a person in a dream" (Woolf, *To the Lighthouse* 59).

From the beginning of the novel, Mr. Ramsay is represented as a sort of tyrant. He provokes fear and anger, especially in his children but sometimes also in Mrs. Ramsay: "He stamped his foot on the stone step. 'Damn you,' he said. But what had she said?" (Woolf, *To the Lighthouse* 29). By acting so strictly and disrespectfully, he tries to hide his constant fear of insignificance. With this front of anger, no one is ever able to see that a man of his sort is capable of showing a softer side. He probably uses this anger to show his power, as he is the important man and everyone should accommodate himself to him. It is not that he does not love his children or want to protect them; it is simply that he wants other people to see him as the powerful man in his family. Therefore, he never actually praises his children until the very end of the novel. "What he said was true, it was always true. He was incapable of untruth" (Woolf, *To the Lighthouse* 8). This rational side seems to be predominant in his words and actions towards his family.

The focus of Woolf's writing was originally on her father, who in many respects is the embodiment of Mr. Ramsay. For this reason, I will now address Virginia Woolf's own family dynamic.

3. Traditional Gender Roles in Virginia Woolf's Life

Virginia Woolf was born in London in 1882 as the third child of Leslie and Julia Stephen. In light of her childhood and parts of her life, it is obvious that she was born into a family that lived according to traditional values.

Woolf describes her parents in an overwhelmingly positive light: "[b]eautiful often, even to our eyes, were their gestures, their glances of pure and unutterable delight in each other." (Liukkonen). To my mind, this clearly shows that her parents were a normal couple who loved each other, and that each of them knew and embodied their particular role. From my perspective, Woolf attempted to reflect her parents somewhat in the Ramsay family, as they also lived according to traditional gender roles. This is why Zwerdling consciously compares Julia Stephen with Mrs. Ramsay: "Like Mrs. Ramsay, Julia Stephen was home- and family- centered, astonishingly beautiful, and selfless almost to a fault." (188).

Woolf's father, Leslie Stephen, was a literary critic, author, and editor. He accepted "the editorship of the *Dictionary of National Biography*, which has come to be seen as his greatest achievement." (Zwerdling 186). This achievement could be the foundation for the lasting argument that he was the man in the house, the successful businessman who brought the money home. Virginia Woolf had to experience a lot with respect to male and female roles in her life. First of all, DeSalvo believes that Woolf was repeatedly raped by her two older half-brothers ("Virginia Woolf" 276). This act of violation is the ultimate display of traditional male domination over women, for the women were hardly capable of defending themselves. Secondly, Woolf could never understand why boys favoured in everything, in contrast to girls. "In later life Virginia would sometimes complain that she was denied the education that was given automatically to boys." (Nicolson).

In the middle ages of her life, Woolf described the period when she was educated at home by her father. In a letter to Vita Sackville-West, she writes: "Think how I was brought up! No school; mooning about alone among my father's books; never any chance to pick up all that goes on in schools—throwing balls; ragging; slang; vulgarities; scenes; jealousies!" (Liukkonen).

4. Lily Briscoe and her own female identity

In contrast to Mrs. Ramsay, Lily is young and unmarried. She is a   painter who befriends the Ramsays. Due to her profession, which is normally dominated by men, she, like Mr. Ramsay, has to struggle with fears that her work lacks worth. The opinions of men like Charles Tansley come close to undermining her confidence. "Charles Tansley used to say, she remembered, women can't paint, can't write." (Woolf, *To the Lighthouse* 132). The problem is her lack of self-confidence to present her own view of the world. She expresses this fear by saying:

> Such she often felt herself - struggling against terrifying odds to maintain her courage; to say: `but this is what I see`, and so to clasp some miserable remnant of her vision to her breast, which a thousand forces did their best to pluck from her. And it was then too, in that chill and windy way, as she began to paint, that they forced themselves upon her other things, in her own inadequacy, her insignificance, keeping house for her father off the Brompton Road, and had much ado to control her impulse to fling herself (thank Heaven she had always resisted so far) at Mrs Ramsay's knee and say to her - but what could one say to her? `I'm in love with you`? No, that was not true. `I'm in love with this all`, waving her hand at the hedge, at the house, at the children? It was absurd, it was impossible. One could not say what one meant. (Woolf, *To the Lighthouse* 19)

Lily is a reserved individual and rejects the traditional model of femininity embodied by Mrs. Ramsay. She is thus Mrs. Ramsay's total opposite, and she loves to be independent and alone. She sees that Mrs. Ramsay always has many friends around her, and she would probably like to have many friends, too. But not in the same way; to my mind, she seems to want something more profound than a friend. On the other hand, Lily loves Mrs. Ramsay, and deeply longs for her beauty and unity. "Could loving, as people called it, make her and Mrs. Ramsay one? for it was not knowledge but unity that she desired" (Woolf, *To the Lighthouse* 44). Although Lily shares some character traits with Mrs. and Mr. Ramsay, she does not want to be like them, nor does she want to behave in the same way as their children and guests. Bowlby interprets Lily's resistance as follows:

> If Mrs. Ramsay endeavours to preserve the spectacle of the composure of feminine and masculine relationships, Lily Briscoe is placed outside this structure, fascinated by it but resisting incorporation into it as a woman who, in Mrs. Ramsay's scheme, should marry Mr. Bankes. (73)

All the issues I have listed about Lily reveal that she is a very doubtful and self-conscious woman. She knows that most females are mothers and loving wives who stay at home and play their traditional role. But Lily does not want to be a traditional woman: she wants something else. Since this longing for something different is so deep in her, she keeps on painting and eventually knows how she can give shape to this formless, chaotic desire. At the end of the novel she gets what she had wished for a very long time: "It was done; it was finished. Yes, she thought, laying down her brush in extreme fatigue, I have had my vision." (Woolf, *To the Lighthouse* 170). Now she is finally assured that a woman, too, can paint and write.

5. Conclusion: Virginia Woolf in comparison to Lily Briscoe

In the process of my research and writing, it has become quite obvious to me that Virginia Woolf tried to mirror herself in the character of Lily Briscoe. Both women are very similar; one could say that they both have new ideas and are very modern. Both women are seeking for something unique, a thing that makes them different from other women. Virginia Woolf successfully separated herself from her parents, just as Lily did from the Ramsays. As Woolf was born into a family that followed traditional gender roles, it is obvious that they would have expected her to act accordingly. In Zwerdling's words: "Born in 1882, [Woolf] was destined to witness and participate in an extraordinary transformation of the ideals of marriage and family life." (145) However, she tried to come to terms with her family; lamenting her parents' death, she clung to her desire for writing, with help neither from her parents nor from society at large. Lily follows the same path with respect to the Ramsay family. Although she really loves them, it is clear that she does not want to be as them. At the end of the novel, she eventually ceases her grieving over Mrs. Ramsay's death and finally finds belief in her ability for painting. Thus, Lily is able to finish her own picture, and in this way she develops a new female identity.

In her book, Suzanne Raitt accurately explains Virginia Woolf's truthful reason for writing this novel: "Woolf saw *To the Lighthouse* as a form of therapy: a text with a peculiar relation to her own history, which functioned for her as a psychical and emotional release." (9). In *To the Lighthouse*, Woolf was able to mirror her own feelings and experiences through Lily Brisoe. On the one hand, of course, she does not have exactly the same personality as Lily; but on the other hand, her true inner feelings and desires are very much reflected in Lily's. In Virginia Woolf's "Modern Fiction", she reveals her plain opinion about the challenge of women in our society using the example of a novelist:

> Life is not a series of gig lamps symmetrically arranged; life is a luminous halo, a semi-transparent envelope surrounding us from the beginning of consciousness to the end. Is it not the task of the novelist to convey this varying, this unknown and uncircumcised spirit, whatever aberration or complexity it may display, with as little mixture of the alien and external as possible? (150)

Today, there are only a few women who do not work and stay at home with their family. Nevertheless, there are men who still regard themselves as superior to women, as more important in society. Therefore, it could be helpful for women to read this kind of book. Through Woolf's testimony, they will see how courageous and tough a woman must sometimes be in order to assert her place in the world.

Works Cited

1. Bowlby, Rachel. *Virginia Woolf*: Feminist Destinations. Oxford. Blackwell, 1988.

2. DeSalvo, Louise. "Virginia Woolf: The Impact of Childhood Sexual Abuse on Her Life and Work." *Women's Studies International Forum* 13.3 (Boston: Beacon Press, 1989).

3. Liukkonen, Petri. "Virginia Woolf (1882-1941) - in full Adeline Virginia Woolf, original surname Stephen". http://www.kirjasto.sci.fi/vwoolf.htm

4. Nicolson, Nigel. *Virginia Woolf. New York Times on the Web.* 2000. http://www.nytimes.com/books/first/n/nicolson-woolf.html?_r=1

5. Raitt, Suzanne. *Virginia Woolf's* To the Lighthouse. New York: St. Martin's Press, 1990.

6. Woolf, Virginia. *To the Lighthouse.* United States. Oxford University Press, 2006.

7. ---. "Modern Fiction". The Common Reader: First Series, ed. Andrew McNeillie (London: Hogarth Press, 1984).

8. Zwerdling, Alex. *Virginia Woolf and the Real World.* Berkley: University of California Press, 1986.